P9-CCF-253

the true book of

Buds

SURPRISE PACKAGES

By Dr. Helen Ross Russell

Educational Associate, Wave Hill Center
for Environmental Studies

Illustrations by John and Lucy Hawkinson

 CHILDRENS PRESS, CHICAGO

To the boys and girls of the city of New York, and to their teachers who explored the surprise packages of their neighborhood with the author and who made many exciting discoveries.

Library of Congress Catalog Card Number: 72-101596

1 2 3 4 5 6 7 8 9 10 11 12 13 14 15 16 17 18 19 20 21 22 23 24 25 R 75 74 73 72 71 70

One winter day Tom brought a twig to school for the children to see.

"Look what I found!" he said. "This twig has buds. Spring must be coming."

All the children looked at Tom's twig.

The twig had a big fat bud at the tip. It had other little buds on the sides.

Jane said, "This is a nice twig. But it does not mean that spring is coming. All twigs have buds."

HORSE CHESTNUT
Enlarged

All the children started to talk. Some thought that all the trees had buds. Some didn't think so. Some were not sure.

"How can we find out?" asked Miss Roberts.

"We could go outside and look at some trees," said Carol.

"There are trees on the playground," said Ted.

The boys and girls put on their coats and hats and boots. They went outside.

They looked at
the big maple tree.
It had buds.

They looked at
the sycamore.
It had buds.

There were evergreen trees near the building.

"Do evergreen trees have buds?" asked Sue.

"Let's look," said Miss Roberts.

The children walked over to the evergreen trees.

"Look," said Jane.
"The pine tree has buds."
All the other evergreens had buds.
The bushes beside the evergreens
had buds, too.

All the trees and
bushes on our school
ground have buds.

When the children went back to their room, they made a chart.

Miss Roberts said, "When you go home, look at the trees along the street. Look at the trees and bushes in the park. Look at the trees and bushes in yards. See if they all have buds."

The next day all the children wanted to talk at once.

"We will take turns," said Miss Roberts.

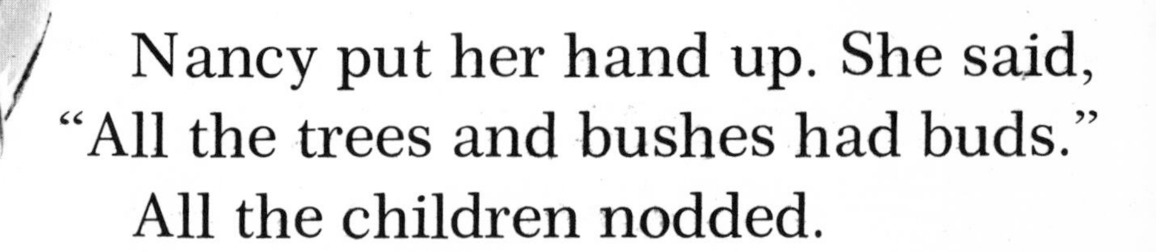

Nancy put her hand up. She said, "All the trees and bushes had buds."

All the children nodded.

Jimmy said, "But they were not all alike."

"How were they different?" asked Miss Roberts.

The children said,
"Some were fat."
"Some were long."
"Some were small."
"Some were green."
"Some were red."
"Some were purple."
"Some were brown."
"Some were shiny."
"Some were fuzzy."
"Some were sticky."
"What is in the buds?"
asked Sam.
"Leaves," said Tom.
"Flowers," said Sue.
"I don't know," said Jane.
"How can we find out?" asked
Miss Roberts.

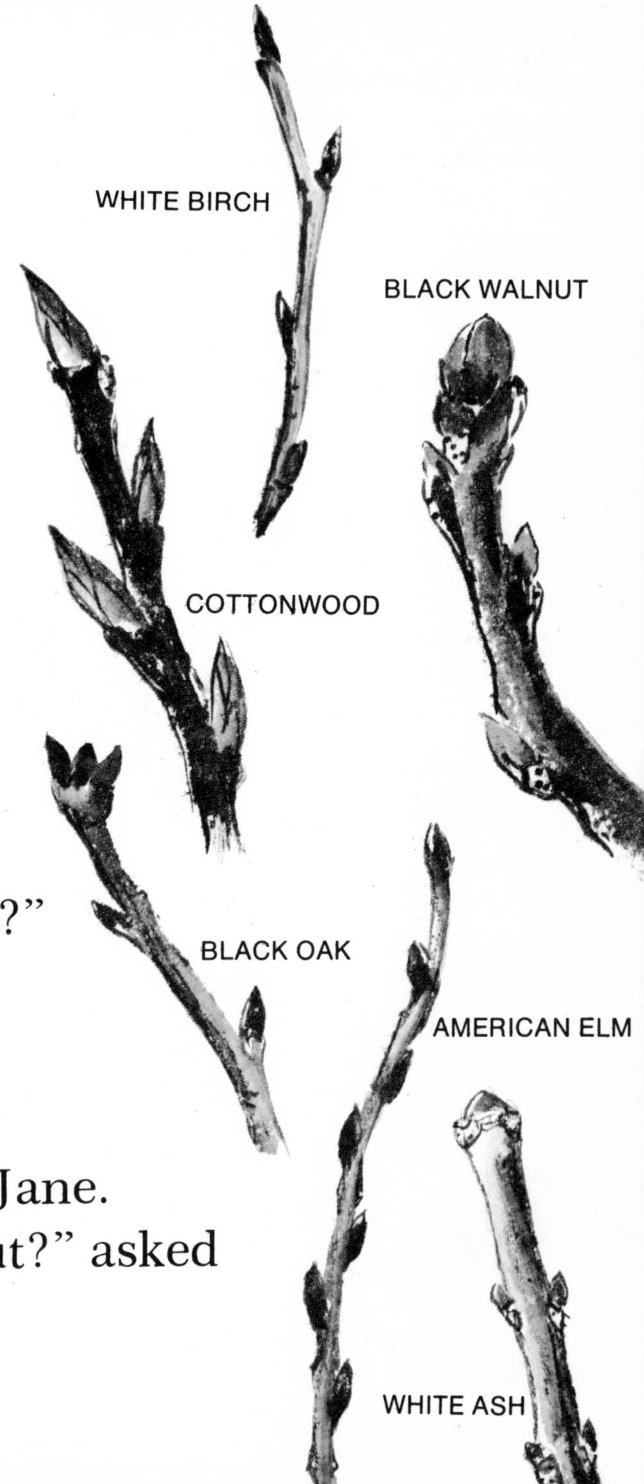

"Wait and see," said Nancy.
"Look inside," said Ted.
"Those are both good ideas," said Miss Roberts. "If you want to know what is in a package, what do you do?"
"Unwrap it," said the children.
"The wrappings on buds are called bud scales," said Miss Roberts. "If we take the scales off we can see what is inside. Let's take the scales off Tom's big bud."
The children took turns. Each child pulled off one scale. The scales were sticky. They stuck to their fingers.
The scales on the outside of the bud were smaller than the inside ones. The inside ones reached from the bottom of the bud to the very tip.

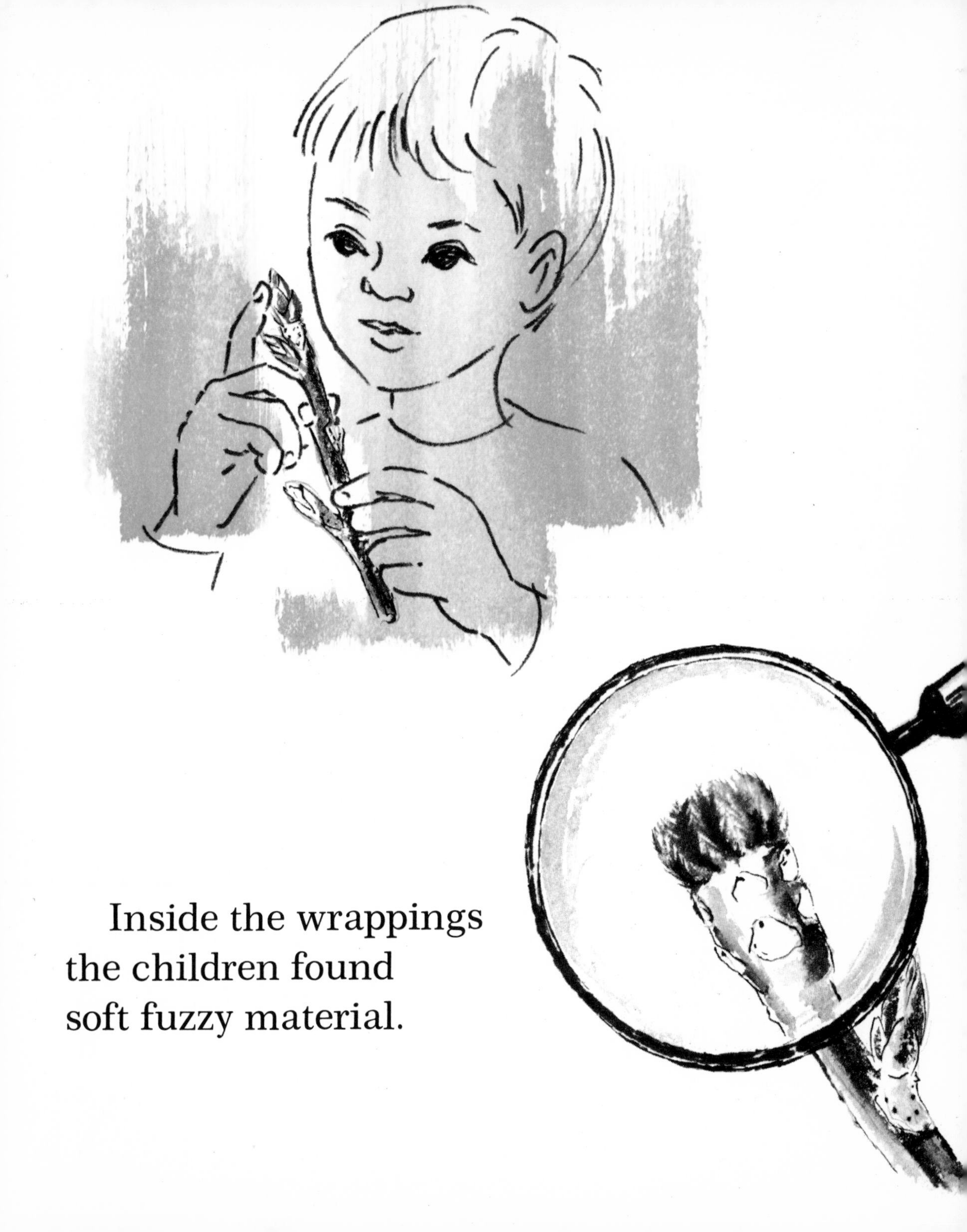

Inside the wrappings
the children found
soft fuzzy material.

Enlarged

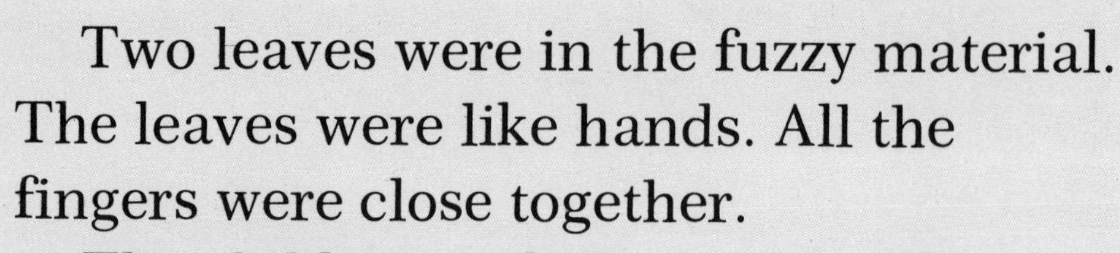

Two leaves were in the fuzzy material. The leaves were like hands. All the fingers were close together.

The children took the leaves off the bud. They found two more leaves inside. These were smaller than the outside leaves. They, too, were covered with fuzz and were folded up.

A little ball was between these two leaves.

"What is it?" asked Carol.

"Flowers," said Sue.

"More leaves," said Ted.

"How can we find out?" asked Miss Roberts.

"Use our hand lens," said Sam.

Jimmy got the hand lens. The children looked at the little ball.

"What do you see?" asked Miss Roberts.

"A lot of little balls," said Ted. "But I don't know what they are."

"I think they are baby flowers," said Sue. "But I am not sure."

"My father says the twig came from our horse chestnut tree," said Tom. "I will watch the tree. When the buds start to open, I will bring some to school. Then we can be sure."

"That's a good idea," said Miss Roberts.

The children thought so, too.

The next day
Miss Roberts brought
buds from a beech
tree to school.

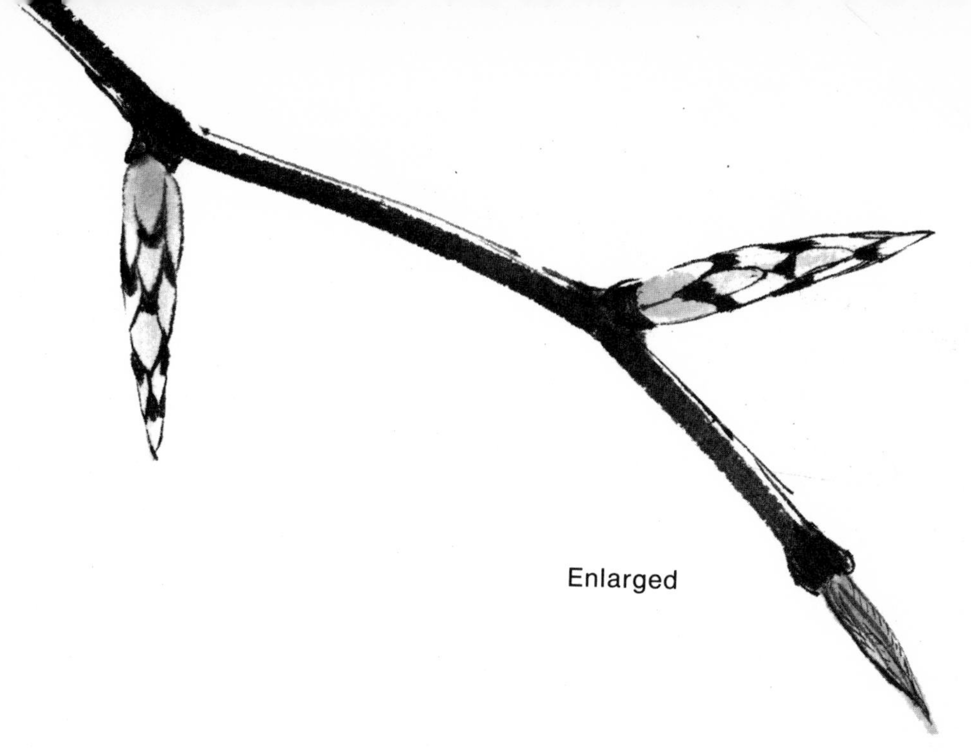
Enlarged

Each child took one apart. When they got the scale wrappings off, they found baby leaves inside.

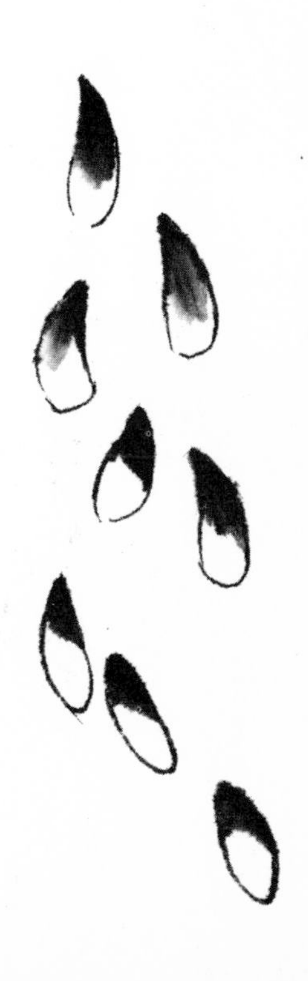

Enlarged

A few days later Jimmy said, "I went to visit my grandmother. I told her about unwrapping bud packages. She gave me this twig from her forsythia bush. She said if we put it in water we would have a surprise."

The children put the forsythia in water. They gave it more water every day. They looked at it every day. A week went by. Nothing happened.

Then one day Jane said, "The buds are getting bigger."

Another week went by. One bud had a bit of yellow showing.

A few days later the buds began to open.

There was one flower in each bud.

One morning Jimmy said, “Look, this bud is different. It has leaves in it.”

The children looked at the leaf buds.

There were two leaves on the outside around two smaller leaves.

“They are packaged just like the horse chestnut leaves,” said Jane.

Carol said, “If we brought apple twigs inside and put them in water would they open, too?”

“I don’t know,” said Miss Roberts. “How can we find out?”

“We could try lots of different kinds of buds,” said Ted.

“That’s a good idea,” said Miss Roberts. “Ask your father or mother to help you cut some twigs so you do not hurt the trees.”

The children brought twigs to school. They put them in water in a sunny window. They watched

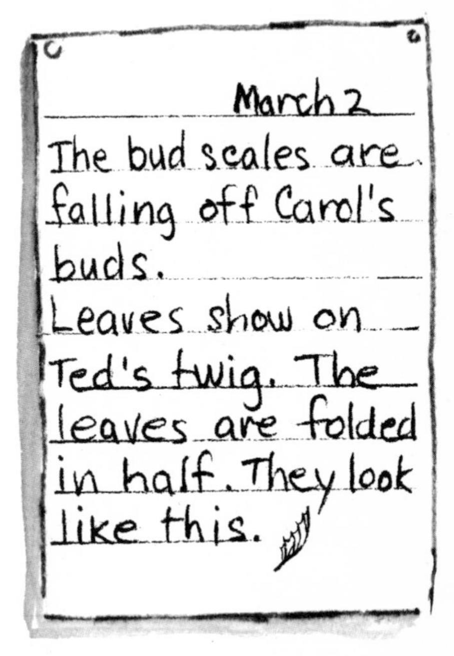

them every day. They made a chart
of what happened.

A few buds opened the first week.
Some buds opened the second week.
More buds opened the third week.
The buds on some twigs never opened at all.

"Look at my apple flowers," said Carol. "They look like doll flowers."

"So do the dogwood flowers," said Jane.

"Why are they so small?" asked Ted.

"They need food to grow," said Miss Roberts. "The apple tree stored extra food in its trunk and roots last summer. When Carol cut the twig off the tree, she took it away from its food supply."

"But the forsythia flowers were big," said Sam.

"Forsythia buds were big when winter came. The flowers were all ready to open," said Miss Roberts.

One day
Jane brought
pussy-willow
branches
to school.

The buds were
gray, silky catkins.

Each bud had
only one scale.

As the bud
grew, the scale
fell off.

Soon the gray
catkins began
to turn yellow.
They were
covered with
yellow dust.
The dust fell
on the window-
sill.

"What is that yellow dust?" asked Tom.

"Pollen," said Miss Roberts.

"Flowers have pollen," said Ted. "Are the willow catkins flowers?"

"Yes," said Miss Roberts.

"Where are the flower petals?" asked Jimmy.

"Many tree flowers have no petals," said Miss Roberts.

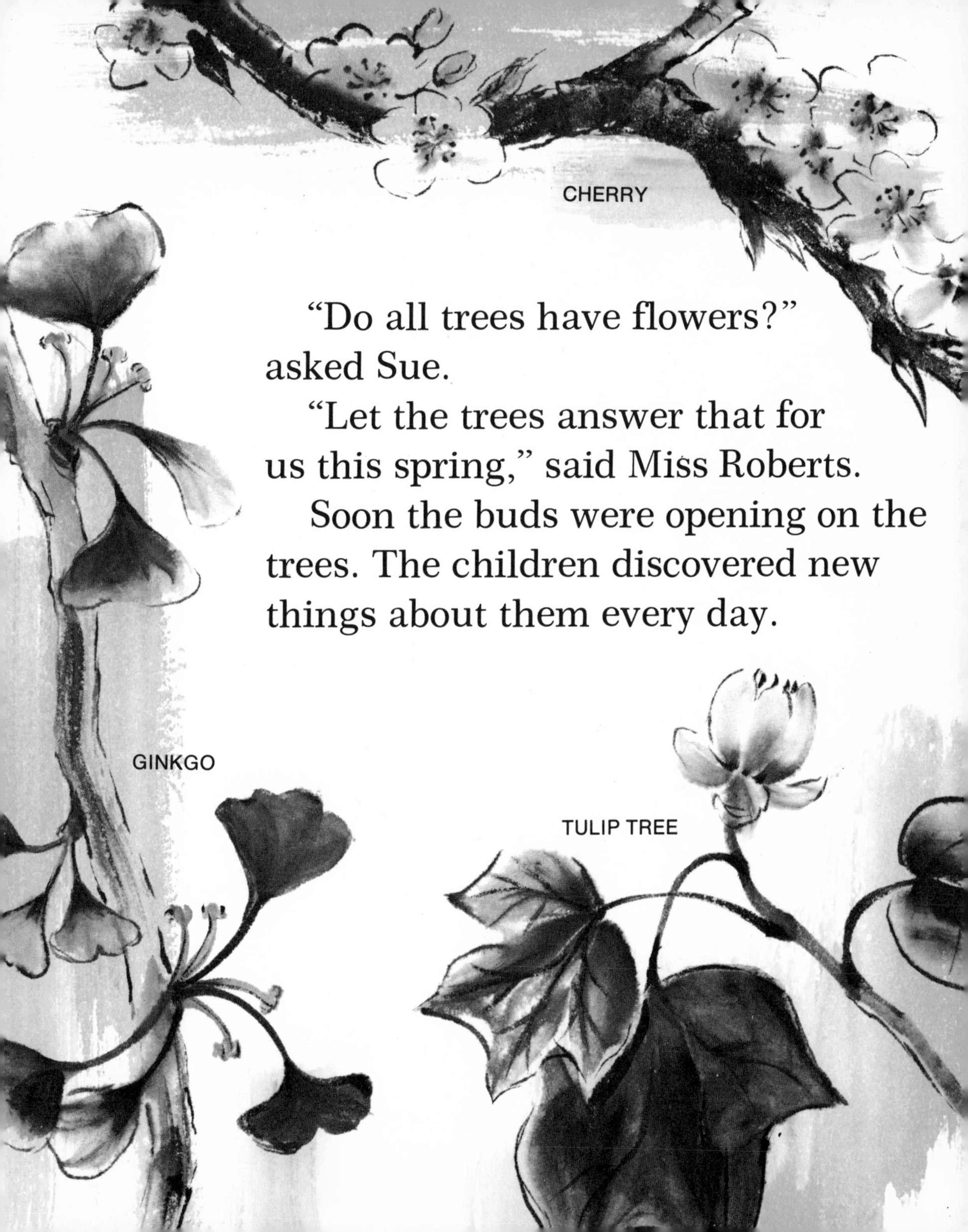

"Do all trees have flowers?" asked Sue.

"Let the trees answer that for us this spring," said Miss Roberts.

Soon the buds were opening on the trees. The children discovered new things about them every day.

MAPLE ST.

"Let's adopt the Norway maple tree on the corner," said Miss Roberts. "We will look at it every day and see how the bud packages open and what they hold."

"We can make a chart for the Norway maple," said Sue.

Our Norway Maple Tree

April 15:

The buds have not started to open.

The buds are reddish.

The buds on the end of the twigs are bigger than the ones on the sides.

The side buds are in pairs.

NORWAY MAPLE
Enlarged 10 Times

One day the Norway maple was covered with flowers.

"We will pick one twig," said Miss Roberts. There are enough flowers on it so every child can have one."

Back in the room, Miss Roberts held the twig for all the children to see. She was standing in the sun. The flowers made a shadow picture on the wall.

"Let's trace shadow pictures," said Jane.

One day Ted brought an oak twig to school. The children were surprised to find pollen-making flowers on it.

They found pollen-making flowers on the spruce tree, too. They found red and purple cones. Miss Roberts said the cones were another kind of spruce flower.

BLACK SPRUCE

Then one day Tom brought a big grocery bag to school. “Look what came out of the horse-chestnut bud package!” he said.

The tiny leaves that had looked like hands had opened and grown big.

The little cluster of balls was a big bunch of beautiful flowers.

“I thought they were flower buds,” said Sue.

HORSE CHESTNUT

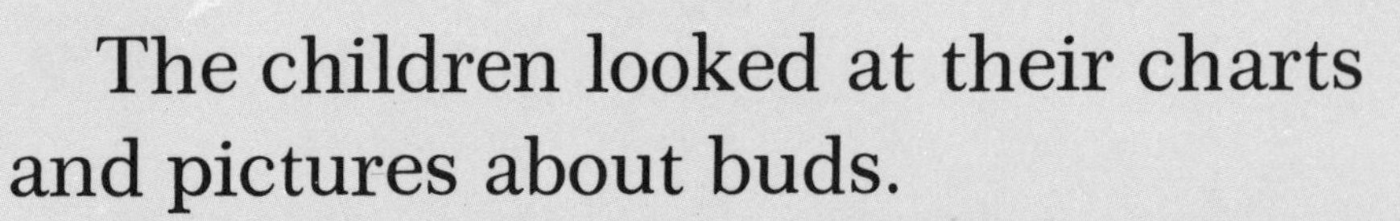

The children looked at their charts and pictures about buds.

"We almost wrote a book," said Ted.

They had written:

BUDS

Buds are packages.
They hold leaves or flowers.
Some buds hold both.
Some flowers are pretty.
Some flowers are only pollen flowers.
Leaves are folded in many different
ways in buds.
It is fun to watch buds opening.
They are like surprise packages.